# THE
# CUSTOMER SERVICE
# POCKETBOOK

By Tony Newby

*Drawings by Alexis Archier*

D0785522

"Down to earth practical guide ... what I would expect from y... ...on Customer Service. It removes a lot of the mystique and concentrates on the real issues."
**Mr. L.J.G. Purdie, Chief Pensions Manager, Scottish Widows.**

# CONTENTS

# WHY CUSTOMER SERVICE MATTERS

**WHY CUSTOMER SERVICE MATTERS**

# CUSTOMER CONTACT

Customer service matters because EVERYBODY in EVERY organisation:

- Either helps customers DIRECTLY
- Or helps INTERNAL CUSTOMERS who in turn directly serve the paying customers

This book is for people who work in:

- Commercial companies, supplying goods or services
- Public sector utilities
- Central and local government departments
- Voluntary organisations

...because they ALL have customers

# WHY CUSTOMER SERVICE MATTERS

## PERSONAL NEEDS

You want:

- To stay in business

- To stay in your job

- To be someone people think of positively

Good customer service equals:

- Commercial survival

- Job security

- Good self-image

### WHY CUSTOMER SERVICE MATTERS

## CUSTOMER EXPECTATIONS

Customers have expectations:

- Often set by other industries, eg banks, airlines, fast food outlets, etc. You are not just competing with businesses that are similar to your own.

- Continually evolving and growing more demanding, so you can never sit back complacently.

Your standards of customer service always need to be on an upward curve.

# WHY CUSTOMER SERVICE MATTERS

## THE IMPORTANCE OF "HOW"

Today, the "How" is as important as the "What"

Competing goods and services don't differ greatly from each other, so the way that you supply them to your customers can become more important than the product or service itself:

- At the point of sale

- In follow-up after-sales

## WHY CUSTOMER SERVICE MATTERS

# REPEAT BUSINESS

If your customer service is merely "adequate" then it is probably INVISIBLE to customers

Adequate service often registers as POOR by comparison with other organisations

Only EXCELLENT service gets noticed!

Repeat business is the life-blood of most businesses:

- Will your customers "write it off to experience" and go elsewhere next time?

OR

- Are you creating a business where customers will WANT to come back?

# WHY CUSTOMER SERVICE MATTERS

## THE "SILENT" COMPLAINER

Most dissatisfied customers don't tell you:

- They tell their friends

- They add embellishments

- It turns into a real horror story - you may even attract hostile press publicity

## WHY CUSTOMER SERVICE MATTERS

# EXERCISE

Here is a short exercise for you to draw on your own experiences of good and bad customer service. It will help you to understand what it is like to be on the receiving end - and you can adapt the lessons to the service you yourself provide in your own job.

Think of one occasion in the last six months when you have received really excellent customer service and one occasion when the service was terrible. Neither example should have anything to do with your present employer. Recall what happened: the things that were said, the tone of voice adopted, the good or bad actions that were carried out.

Complete the "Good Experience" and "Bad Experience" reviews on the following pages and then compare what you have written with the commentary that follows.

## EXERCISE
## My Own Experiences of EXCELLENT Customer Service

1. The company/organisation I was dealing with?

. . . . . . . . . . . . . . . . . . . . . . . . . . . . . . . . . . . . . . . . . . . . . . . . . . . . . . . . . . . . . . . . . . . . . . . . .

2. How was I greeted?

. . . . . . . . . . . . . . . . . . . . . . . . . . . . . . . . . . . . . . . . . . . . . . . . . . . . . . . . . . . . . . . . . . . . . . . . .

3. How promptly was I attended to?

. . . . . . . . . . . . . . . . . . . . . . . . . . . . . . . . . . . . . . . . . . . . . . . . . . . . . . . . . . . . . . . . . . . . . . . . .

4. How do I think I was regarded by the person serving me?

. . . . . . . . . . . . . . . . . . . . . . . . . . . . . . . . . . . . . . . . . . . . . . . . . . . . . . . . . . . . . . . . . . . . . . . . .

5. What effect (if any) did the way you were served have on how you personally felt at the time?

. . . . . . . . . . . . . . . . . . . . . . . . . . . . . . . . . . . . . . . . . . . . . . . . . . . . . . . . . . . . . . . . . . . . . . . . .

## EXERCISE
### My Own Experiences of EXCELLENT Customer Service (contd)

6. Did you get what you wanted from the transaction?

. . . . . . . . . . . . . . . . . . . . . . . . . . . . . . . . . . . . . . . . . . . . . . . . . . . . . . . . . . . . . . . . . . . . . . . .

7. Has that experience affected your subsequent dealings with that company/organisation?

. . . . . . . . . . . . . . . . . . . . . . . . . . . . . . . . . . . . . . . . . . . . . . . . . . . . . . . . . . . . . . . . . . . . . . . .

8. Name three companies that have a good reputation:

. . . . . . . . . . . . . . . . . . . . . . . . . . . . . . . . . . . . . . . . . . . . . . . . . . . . . . . . . . . . . . . . . . . . . . . .

. . . . . . . . . . . . . . . . . . . . . . . . . . . . . . . . . . . . . . . . . . . . . . . . . . . . . . . . . . . . . . . . . . . . . . . .

9. What gives a company a good name?

. . . . . . . . . . . . . . . . . . . . . . . . . . . . . . . . . . . . . . . . . . . . . . . . . . . . . . . . . . . . . . . . . . . . . . . .

## EXERCISE
**My Own Experiences of POOR Customer Service**

1. The company/organisation I was dealing with?

. . . . . . . . . . . . . . . . . . . . . . . . . . . . . . . . . . . . . . . . . . . . . . . . . . . . . . . . . . . . . . . . . . . . . . . .

2. How was I greeted?

. . . . . . . . . . . . . . . . . . . . . . . . . . . . . . . . . . . . . . . . . . . . . . . . . . . . . . . . . . . . . . . . . . . . . . . .

3. How promptly was I attended to?

. . . . . . . . . . . . . . . . . . . . . . . . . . . . . . . . . . . . . . . . . . . . . . . . . . . . . . . . . . . . . . . . . . . . . . . .

4. How do I think I was regarded by the person serving me?

. . . . . . . . . . . . . . . . . . . . . . . . . . . . . . . . . . . . . . . . . . . . . . . . . . . . . . . . . . . . . . . . . . . . . . . .

5. What effect (if any) did the way you were served have on how you personally felt at the time?

. . . . . . . . . . . . . . . . . . . . . . . . . . . . . . . . . . . . . . . . . . . . . . . . . . . . . . . . . . . . . . . . . . . . . . . .

## EXERCISE
**My Own Experiences of POOR Customer Service (contd)**

6. Did you get what you wanted from the transaction?

. . . . . . . . . . . . . . . . . . . . . . . . . . . . . . . . . . . . . . . . . . . . . . . . . . . . . . . . . . . . . . . . . . . . . . . . . . .

7. Has that experience affected your subsequent dealings with that company/organisation?

. . . . . . . . . . . . . . . . . . . . . . . . . . . . . . . . . . . . . . . . . . . . . . . . . . . . . . . . . . . . . . . . . . . . . . . . . . .

8. Name three companies that have a poor reputation:

. . . . . . . . . . . . . . . . . . . . . . . . . . . . . . . . . . . . . . . . . . . . . . . . . . . . . . . . . . . . . . . . . . . . . . . . . . .

. . . . . . . . . . . . . . . . . . . . . . . . . . . . . . . . . . . . . . . . . . . . . . . . . . . . . . . . . . . . . . . . . . . . . . . . . . .

9. What gives a company a bad name?

. . . . . . . . . . . . . . . . . . . . . . . . . . . . . . . . . . . . . . . . . . . . . . . . . . . . . . . . . . . . . . . . . . . . . . . . . . .

## COMMENTS ON THE EXERCISE

2. How was I greeted?
   eg: warmly; with indifference; aggressively; in an over-familiar tone; cold politeness; etc.

3. How promptly was I attended to?
   eg: Immediately; kept waiting while the assistant chatted; kept waiting because of the queue; etc.

4. How do I think I was regarded by the person serving me?
   eg: As a nuisance; as a "punter" to be sold something (anything); as a valued customer; etc.

5. What effect (if any) did the way you were served have on how you personally felt at the time?
   eg: You felt pleased; valued; annoyed; frustrated; powerless; etc.

7. Has that experience affected your subsequent dealings with that company/organisation?
   eg: Have you told the company about your (good or bad) experience?; have you stopped shopping there?; etc.

(13)

14

# WHAT'S DIFFERENT ABOUT GOOD SERVICE?

## WHAT'S DIFFERENT ABOUT GOOD SERVICE?

# LEARNING

Customer service is a mixture of

● Knowledge

AND

● Skills

Nobody is born with this knowledge or skill

Good customer service is something that is learned, quickly and easily, by anyone who wants to carry out his or her work in a professional manner

**WHAT'S DIFFERENT ABOUT GOOD SERVICE?**

# KNOWLEDGE

Good customer service reflects thorough knowledge of:

- The products or services you supply

- The external customers for those products and services

- The systems and procedures of your organisation

- The network of internal customers with whom you work

# CUSTOMER SERVICE SKILLS

Good customer service reflects competence in certain essential skills:

- Getting it right the first time

- Listening to customers

- Handling complaints in a constructive way

- Being assertive when under pressure

- Communicating clearly

- Making it easier for your colleagues to help customers

## WHAT'S DIFFERENT ABOUT GOOD SERVICE?

# CORPORATE CULTURE

Good customer service reflects the whole corporate culture

Good customer service is based upon not just the knowledge and skills of the individual but also upon the way that the organisation as a whole, from top management downwards, pulls in the same direction and presents a clear, positive message to customers

This reflects:

- Policies - clear corporate standards of quality and behaviour, linked to consistent marketing messages (what the organisation promises, it must deliver!)
- Administrative procedures - that do not sabotage the best efforts of employees to be responsive to customers
- Management style - that actively rewards good customer service behaviour by employees - that does not allow short-term panics to undermine long-term credibility

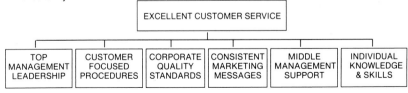

EXCELLENT CUSTOMER SERVICE

| TOP MANAGEMENT LEADERSHIP | CUSTOMER FOCUSED PROCEDURES | CORPORATE QUALITY STANDARDS | CONSISTENT MARKETING MESSAGES | MIDDLE MANAGEMENT SUPPORT | INDIVIDUAL KNOWLEDGE & SKILLS |

### WHAT'S DIFFERENT ABOUT GOOD SERVICE?

## QUALITY

Good customer service is NOT a smile campaign! It is about:

● The quality of what you deliver

AND

● The quality of how you deliver it

Good customer service is based upon the very basic truth that you cannot survive by taking a short-term view of your customers - if they don't come back, if their friends, relations and acquaintances don't come back, there is no future

## WHAT'S DIFFERENT ABOUT GOOD SERVICE?

# ATTENTION TO DETAIL

Everybody has to work at customer service to get it right

BUT

Most of the improvements needed to achieve excellent customer service require very small changes in the way we work day-to-day, not mega-projects to change the universe

GOOD CUSTOMER SERVICE IS THE PRODUCT OF CLOSE ATTENTION TO IMPORTANT SMALL DETAILS

## QUIZ
### How Customer-Friendly Are You?

1. If customers do not complain, does that mean   everyone is doing a great job?

. . . . . . . . . . . . . . . . . . . . . . . . . . . . . . . . . . . . . . . . . . . . . . . . . . . . . . . . . . . . . . . . . . . . . . . . . . . .

. . . . . . . . . . . . . . . . . . . . . . . . . . . . . . . . . . . . . . . . . . . . . . . . . . . . . . . . . . . . . . . . . . . . . . . . . . . .

2. A medium-sized or large organisation will have thousands or even tens of thousands of customers: does it matter if it loses one dissatisfied customer?

. . . . . . . . . . . . . . . . . . . . . . . . . . . . . . . . . . . . . . . . . . . . . . . . . . . . . . . . . . . . . . . . . . . . . . . . . . . .

. . . . . . . . . . . . . . . . . . . . . . . . . . . . . . . . . . . . . . . . . . . . . . . . . . . . . . . . . . . . . . . . . . . . . . . . . . . .

3. How do you think customers feel about organisations that deal constructively with their complaints?

. . . . . . . . . . . . . . . . . . . . . . . . . . . . . . . . . . . . . . . . . . . . . . . . . . . . . . . . . . . . . . . . . . . . . . . . . . . .

. . . . . . . . . . . . . . . . . . . . . . . . . . . . . . . . . . . . . . . . . . . . . . . . . . . . . . . . . . . . . . . . . . . . . . . . . . . .

## QUIZ
### How Customer-Friendly Are You? (continued)

4. "If we make it difficult for complaints to get through, they'll give up". What do you think?

. . . . . . . . . . . . . . . . . . . . . . . . . . . . . . . . . . . . . . . . . . . . . . . . . . . . . . . . . . . . . . .

. . . . . . . . . . . . . . . . . . . . . . . . . . . . . . . . . . . . . . . . . . . . . . . . . . . . . . . . . . . . . . .

5. Who are my customers?

. . . . . . . . . . . . . . . . . . . . . . . . . . . . . . . . . . . . . . . . . . . . . . . . . . . . . . . . . . . . . . .

. . . . . . . . . . . . . . . . . . . . . . . . . . . . . . . . . . . . . . . . . . . . . . . . . . . . . . . . . . . . . . .

6. Does this organisation that I work for have any laid-down standards or guidance on how to provide good customer service? List any that you know of.

. . . . . . . . . . . . . . . . . . . . . . . . . . . . . . . . . . . . . . . . . . . . . . . . . . . . . . . . . . . . . . .

. . . . . . . . . . . . . . . . . . . . . . . . . . . . . . . . . . . . . . . . . . . . . . . . . . . . . . . . . . . . . . .

### WHAT'S DIFFERENT ABOUT GOOD SERVICE?

# COMMENTS ON THE QUIZ

1. This is a very risky assumption. In fact, only a minority of dissatisfied customers take the trouble to complain to the company. Many more simply stop using your products or services. And even those who do not complain to the company will undoubtedly complain to their family and friends.

2. Yes - one dissatisfied customer may spread his or her bad feelings to scores of other people. Remember, too, that everyone who stops doing business with you represents not just the loss of one transaction today but the potential loss of a lifetime of such transactions. Just one shopper, buying one loaf of bread a day, would spend £5,000 over a twenty year period (and that ignores price increases).

3. It may seem surprising, but evidence suggests that customers who have had a complaint dealt with efficiently and courteously often become the most loyal customers of all. The reason is actually quite simple: they appreciate the personal attention and care that has been put into responding to their complaint.

## WHAT'S DIFFERENT ABOUT GOOD SERVICE?

## COMMENTS ON THE QUIZ (contd)

4. You can gain a brief escape from complaints if your switchboard is continually jammed, or the "right" person is always unavailable. But sooner or later the customer will win - perhaps in dramatic form, when you find yourself profiled on TV or the company chairman is asked embarrassing questions at the AGM or (for public sector organisations) someone writes to their MP. What is more, the harder you make it for the complainant to get through, the more steamed up and the less inclined to compromise that person will be.

5. You need to know who your external customers are - the people who want your goods or services - and also who your internal customers are - your colleagues who form links in the customer service chain.

6. If you have any doubts about the answer to this question, discuss it with your supervisor or manager.

# PERFORMANCE STANDARDS

## PERFORMANCE STANDARDS

# KEY ELEMENTS

Standards provide two key elements in the customer service system:
- A yardstick by which the quality of customer service can be measured
- Guidance on how particular elements of customer service are to be delivered day-to-day in your job

Standards are usually developed by:

- Managers and personnel specialists who analyse job tasks and determine what the appropriate standard of performance should be
- Trainers who establish standards as a part of training in job skills
- Employees themselves, typically when they are active in quality improvement groups of one kind or another

And, of course, standards reflect the levels of expectation that other organisations are creating amongst your own customers

## PERFORMANCE STANDARDS

## EXAMPLES

Most of these examples of Performance Standards will apply in your own organisation; some may need adapting; and there may well be other standards that are unique to your situation:

**Standard 1:** Right first time - tasks (or parts of tasks) are completed correctly, so that work does not have to be returned for corrective action

**Standard 2:** When something is promised to a customer, the promise must be realistic, it must be kept, and any unforeseen and unavoidable delays must be notified

**Standard 3:** When you "inherit" errors that have been passed on from elsewhere in the organisation, you will not pass those errors on to others (this may require that you return the incorrect work, or that you refer it to your supervisor or manager)

**Standard 4:** All written work must be clear and understandable (this may require that your organisation agrees a set of style rules for all documents and correspondence, covering such matters as jargon, sentence complexity, obligation to give clear explanations, and the like)

## PERFORMANCE STANDARDS

## EXAMPLES (contd)

**Standard 5:** Both internal and external customers should at all times be treated with the maximum courtesy and helpfulness

**Standard 6:** Records, correspondence, and files should be left in a state such that they could be easily dealt with by someone other than the person who normally handles those items

**Standard 7:** All telephones should be answered within three rings and the person answering should give his or her name and department (some organisations may opt for four rings, until improvements can be achieved, but note that others already operate a standard of two rings maximum before answering)

**Standard 8:** Identify the information needs of internal and external customers and provide that information at the time it is needed

## EXERCISE

For each of the customer service performance standards listed in the previous two pages write down how that standard would apply to the job you yourself do. You may find it useful afterwards to talk to your supervisor about the answers you have written down - and about their implications for how work gets done in your part of the organisation.

How **Standard 1** applies to my work:

. . . . . . . . . . . . . . . . . . . . . . . . . . . . . . . . . . . . . . . . . . . . . . . . . . . . . . . . . . . . . . . . . . . . . . . . . . . . . . .

. . . . . . . . . . . . . . . . . . . . . . . . . . . . . . . . . . . . . . . . . . . . . . . . . . . . . . . . . . . . . . . . . . . . . . . . . . . . . . .

How **Standard 2** applies to my work:

. . . . . . . . . . . . . . . . . . . . . . . . . . . . . . . . . . . . . . . . . . . . . . . . . . . . . . . . . . . . . . . . . . . . . . . . . . . . . . .

. . . . . . . . . . . . . . . . . . . . . . . . . . . . . . . . . . . . . . . . . . . . . . . . . . . . . . . . . . . . . . . . . . . . . . . . . . . . . . .

How **Standard 3** applies to my work:

. . . . . . . . . . . . . . . . . . . . . . . . . . . . . . . . . . . . . . . . . . . . . . . . . . . . . . . . . . . . . . . . . . . . . . . . . . . . . . .

. . . . . . . . . . . . . . . . . . . . . . . . . . . . . . . . . . . . . . . . . . . . . . . . . . . . . . . . . . . . . . . . . . . . . . . . . . . . . . .

How **Standard 4** applies to my work:

. . . . . . . . . . . . . . . . . . . . . . . . . . . . . . . . . . . . . . . . . . . . . . . . . . . . . . . . . . . . . . . . . . . . . . . . . . . . . . .

. . . . . . . . . . . . . . . . . . . . . . . . . . . . . . . . . . . . . . . . . . . . . . . . . . . . . . . . . . . . . . . . . . . . . . . . . . . . . . .

## EXERCISE (CONTINUED)

How **Standard 5** applies to my work:

. . . . . . . . . . . . . . . . . . . . . . . . . . . . . . . . . . . . . . . . . . . . . . . . . . . . . . . . . . . . . . . . . . . . .

. . . . . . . . . . . . . . . . . . . . . . . . . . . . . . . . . . . . . . . . . . . . . . . . . . . . . . . . . . . . . . . . . . . . .

How **Standard 6** applies to my work:

. . . . . . . . . . . . . . . . . . . . . . . . . . . . . . . . . . . . . . . . . . . . . . . . . . . . . . . . . . . . . . . . . . . . .

. . . . . . . . . . . . . . . . . . . . . . . . . . . . . . . . . . . . . . . . . . . . . . . . . . . . . . . . . . . . . . . . . . . . .

How **Standard 7** applies to my work:

. . . . . . . . . . . . . . . . . . . . . . . . . . . . . . . . . . . . . . . . . . . . . . . . . . . . . . . . . . . . . . . . . . . . .

. . . . . . . . . . . . . . . . . . . . . . . . . . . . . . . . . . . . . . . . . . . . . . . . . . . . . . . . . . . . . . . . . . . . .

How **Standard 8** applies to my work:

. . . . . . . . . . . . . . . . . . . . . . . . . . . . . . . . . . . . . . . . . . . . . . . . . . . . . . . . . . . . . . . . . . . . .

. . . . . . . . . . . . . . . . . . . . . . . . . . . . . . . . . . . . . . . . . . . . . . . . . . . . . . . . . . . . . . . . . . . . .

# TURN COMPLAINTS INTO OPPORTUNITIES

# CUSTOMER NEEDS

Most customers who have a complaint about something your organisation has done, or failed to do, simply want the matter put right

In the case of a purchase that has in some way gone wrong, they also want the reassurance that they did not make a bad decision in the first place

Most customers only become irritated, angry or even abusive when their initial attempts to get the matter put right have led them nowhere

**TURN COMPLAINTS INTO OPPORTUNITIES**

## CUSTOMER HELP

How you can help customers get what they want:

- Always respond promptly and helpfully

- Don't let reasonable complaints escalate into life-and-death dramas!

- Once the problem has been sorted out, reassure the customer about the qualities of the product or service your organisation provides (this is made much easier and more credible by the excellent manner in which you have just dealt with the complaint!)

## TURN COMPLAINTS INTO OPPORTUNITIES

# BENEFITS OF COMPLAINTS

Customer complaints offer an opportunity to prevent complaints: ideally, the same complaint should never occur more than once, because the cause of it has been eliminated (the Right First Time standard again) through:

- Improved procedures

- Elimination of product defects

- More skillful customer service behaviour

- Higher performance standards

- Customer-focused management

# TURN COMPLAINTS INTO OPPORTUNITIES

## LIFE-TIME VALUE

When customers have their complaints resolved satisfactorily, they tend to become stronger long-term customers than people who have not had reason to complain. The reason is simple: they are won over by the care and attention given to their complaint - and by the way that this contrasts refreshingly with the indifference, defensiveness, or outright hostility that greets customer complaints in dinosaur organisations (those on the brink of becoming extinct).

What is a customer worth to your organisation over that individual's lifetime? It is a fairly easy exercise to calculate - and the results can be startling, showing just how important it is that not one customer is lost through poor service.

## EXERCISE: LIFE-TIME VALUE OF CUSTOMERS

1. How often (in days, weeks, months or years) does a typical customer make a purchase of the kind of goods or services that your company sells? (Count all occasions, even if sometimes these are sales made to that person by your competitors).

. . . . . . . . . .

2. In a typical lifetime, from say age 25 to age 65, how many purchases does that add up to?

. . . . . . . . . .

3. What is the average (approximate) profit on each sale (at today's prices)?

. . . . . . . . . .

4. Multiply the number of purchases shown in (2) by the profit margin of each sale shown in (3) to arrive at the total life-time value to the business of an average customer (at today's prices):

. . . . . . . .

5. Discuss with your supervisor or manager the life-time value that you have arrived at - and whether or not it represents a sum significant enough to justify efforts to improve the quality of customer service and the prevention and handling of complaints (for some typical areas in which improvements can be found, see the list on the next page)

## EXERCISE: COMMON CAUSES OF COMPLAINTS

Reflect on each of these potential causes of customer dissatisfaction. Make brief notes under each heading, describing examples of these sources of complaint that you are aware of in your own organisation.

1. Products or services that do not live up to the expectations of the purchaser

. . . . . . . . . . . . . . . . . . . . . . . . . . . . . . . . . . . . . . . . . . . . . . . . . . . . . . . . . . . . . . . . . . . . . . . . . .

. . . . . . . . . . . . . . . . . . . . . . . . . . . . . . . . . . . . . . . . . . . . . . . . . . . . . . . . . . . . . . . . . . . . . . . . . .

2. Limited choices, especially in respect of when and how services are delivered to the customer

. . . . . . . . . . . . . . . . . . . . . . . . . . . . . . . . . . . . . . . . . . . . . . . . . . . . . . . . . . . . . . . . . . . . . . . . . .

. . . . . . . . . . . . . . . . . . . . . . . . . . . . . . . . . . . . . . . . . . . . . . . . . . . . . . . . . . . . . . . . . . . . . . . . . .

3. Mistakes

. . . . . . . . . . . . . . . . . . . . . . . . . . . . . . . . . . . . . . . . . . . . . . . . . . . . . . . . . . . . . . . . . . . . . . . . . .

. . . . . . . . . . . . . . . . . . . . . . . . . . . . . . . . . . . . . . . . . . . . . . . . . . . . . . . . . . . . . . . . . . . . . . . . . .

# EXERCISE (CONTD): COMMON CAUSES OF COMPLAINTS

4. Poor external communications, especially when trying to get through to the company, which lead to customer frustration

. . . . . . . . . . . . . . . . . . . . . . . . . . . . . . . . . . . . . . . . . . . . . . . . . . . . . . . . . . . . . . . . . . . . . . . . . . . .

. . . . . . . . . . . . . . . . . . . . . . . . . . . . . . . . . . . . . . . . . . . . . . . . . . . . . . . . . . . . . . . . . . . . . . . . . . . .

5. Poor internal communications, within the company, which create the impression that nobody knows what they are doing, nobody is responsible for anything, and nobody cares anyway

. . . . . . . . . . . . . . . . . . . . . . . . . . . . . . . . . . . . . . . . . . . . . . . . . . . . . . . . . . . . . . . . . . . . . . . . . . . .

. . . . . . . . . . . . . . . . . . . . . . . . . . . . . . . . . . . . . . . . . . . . . . . . . . . . . . . . . . . . . . . . . . . . . . . . . . . .

6. Delays in promised deliveries or in responding to enquiries

. . . . . . . . . . . . . . . . . . . . . . . . . . . . . . . . . . . . . . . . . . . . . . . . . . . . . . . . . . . . . . . . . . . . . . . . . . . .

. . . . . . . . . . . . . . . . . . . . . . . . . . . . . . . . . . . . . . . . . . . . . . . . . . . . . . . . . . . . . . . . . . . . . . . . . . . .

7. Unprofessional behaviour such as indifference or rudeness (it does not matter whether it is intentional or not, if the customer sees it that way)

. . . . . . . . . . . . . . . . . . . . . . . . . . . . . . . . . . . . . . . . . . . . . . . . . . . . . . . . . . . . . . . . . . . . . . . . . . . .

. . . . . . . . . . . . . . . . . . . . . . . . . . . . . . . . . . . . . . . . . . . . . . . . . . . . . . . . . . . . . . . . . . . . . . . . . . . .

## EXERCISE (CONTD): REMOVING COMMON CAUSES OF COMPLAINTS

Go back over the list you've just worked through and jot down brief notes about what (a) needs to be done to prevent the problem happening again and (b) what you think you yourself can do about it. Discuss your answers with your manager.

1. Products or services that do not live up to the expectations of the purchaser

(a)...............................................................................................................

(b)...............................................................................................................
2. Limited choices, especially in respect of when and how services are delivered to the customer

(a)...............................................................................................................

(b)...............................................................................................................
3. Mistakes

(a)...............................................................................................................

(b)...............................................................................................................

## EXERCISE (CONTD): REMOVING COMMON CAUSES OF COMPLAINTS

4. Poor external communications, especially when trying to get through to the company, which lead to customer frustration

(a). . . . . . . . . . . . . . . . . . . . . . . .

(b). . . . . . . . . . . . . . . . . . . . . . . .

5. Poor internal communications, within the company, which create the impression that nobody knows what they are doing, nobody is responsible for anything, and nobody cares

(a). . . . . . . . . . . . . . . . . . . . . . . .

(b). . . . . . . . . . . . . . . . . . . . . . . .

6. Delays in promised deliveries or in responding to enquiries

(a). . . . . . . . . . . . . . . . . . . . . . . .

(b). . . . . . . . . . . . . . . . . . . . . . . .

7. Unprofessional behaviour such as indifference or rudeness (it does not matter whether it is intentional or not, if the customer sees it that way)

(a). . . . . . . . . . . . . . . . . . . . . . . .

(b). . . . . . . . . . . . . . . . . . . . . . . .

**TURN COMPLAINTS INTO OPPORTUNITIES**

# HANDLING COMPLAINTS

1. Identify yourself and always offer to help - never use the blocking excuse that "it's not my job/my department"

2. If a transfer to another telephone extension is absolutely unavoidable (it's better to ensure the right person rings the customer back) then explain what you are doing, minimise the time the customer is on hold, and give the person to whom you are transferring the call all the information you have collected so far

3. Don't get defensive or argue about complaints - agree that the problem exists and put yourself on their side: "Let's see what we can do to sort this out"; politely obtain the customer's name - and use it

4. Don't tell them what you can't do for them, emphasise what you can do

# TURN COMPLAINTS INTO OPPORTUNITIES

## HANDLING COMPLAINTS (contd)

5. Ask for the facts - **check** that you've heard them accurately - and try not to jump to conclusions before you have all the information

6. Admit mistakes and apologise for them; resist the urge to blame other departments or the computer or "company policy" (let the customer go on believing that he or she is dealing with one, unified organisation and not a medieval battleground of warring fiefdoms!)

7. Avoid technical or professional jargon, or references to other departments by initials that are meaningless to outsiders - clear, plain English is the basis of successful communication

8. Only make promises about matters on which **you** personally can deliver

# LISTENING TO CUSTOMERS

**LISTENING TO CUSTOMERS**

# LISTENING SKILLS

If you are to

- Give customers what they want on a right first time basis, or

- Put right something that has gone wrong, or

- Work effectively with your colleagues,

then you need to develop the skills of accurate listening

**LISTENING TO CUSTOMERS**

## LISTENING SKILLS
### 80 : 20 RATIO

1. Effective listening means not talking

- They talk, you listen - the ratio should be 80 : 20 or even 90 : 10

- You don't interrupt (unless they are way off the subject, or you are failing to understand what they are saying)

- You pay attention to what they are saying, rather than sitting there pretending to listen whilst you silently plan your next statement or question

- You make written notes of key points

## LISTENING SKILLS
**CHECK UNDERSTANDING**

2. Check out that you have understood what has been said

- Ask questions to clarify anything you are unsure about

- From time to time give a reflective summary, which briefly paraphrases what the other person has been saying: that way, you both know that you are on common ground

- Don't "tune out" the things that you might be less pleased to hear

## LISTENING SKILLS
**DEMONSTRATE LISTENING**

3. Demonstrate that you are listening, by means of your:

- Eye contact - maintain frequent contact, without giving the impression of a fixed stare

- Body posture - be comfortable, not stiff; open rather than with defensively-crossed arms; lean slightly towards the person, without threatening their sense of personal "territory"

- Interested tone of voice - whatever the words you use, if you don't mean what you say, your tone will give away to the other person that you are not sincere

## LISTENING TO CUSTOMERS

## LISTENING SKILLS
**BUILD RELATIONSHIPS**

4. Build the relationship with the other person

- Give them space to let off steam if they need to, before you move into a problem-solving mode

- Show that you can see things from their point of view

- Use the other person's name

- Focus upon positive action for the future, rather than raking over history

- Include them as contributors to your planned actions - "We can sort this out together..."

## **LISTENING SKILLS**
**DIAGNOSTIC LISTENING**

5. Treat listening as a diagnostic process

- Where errors have occurred, resist the urge to argue, to defend, or to excuse
- Admit mistakes and apologise sincerely, even if you personally had nothing to do with causing the problem - as far as a customer is concerned, you are the representative of everybody in the organisation
- Even if the request or the problem sounds familiar, don't jump to conclusions until you have gathered all the facts
- Look for solutions, not obstacles - the "can do's" which genuinely do impress customers hardened by a lifetime of delays and evasions from dinosaur organisations

## LISTENING TO CUSTOMERS

## EXERCISE

This is both fun to do and may surprise and challenge your view of yourself as a good listener. Get together with a couple of other people, so that each person can test how well he or she listens and to learn from that experience. Each of you will in turn take the role of Speaker, Listener and Observer. Firstly decide the order you want to go in.

Each of you must think of a topic about which that person has quite strong views. The topic must have nothing to do with the organisation in which you work, nor should the topic be selected merely because of its capacity to offend. Rather than being technical, it should be about general knowledge or current affairs to which some degree of controversy attaches (eg "I believe all cars should be banned to protect the environment"). However, it is important that each person sincerely holds a firm viewpoint on the topic he or she selects; otherwise the exercise is pointless.

At the start of each of the three sessions, the person who has the role of Listener will tell the Speaker what the Listener's choice of topic is and the direction in which his or her beliefs lie.

## LISTENING TO CUSTOMERS

## EXERCISE (contd)

The Speaker then argues for not more than five minutes the case against that point of view. The Speaker's task is to argue convincingly (and not abusively) against the Listener's point of view, presenting the benefits of an alternative position and/or demolishing the position that the Listener would normally adopt.

The task of the Listener is to listen accurately (using the rules outlined in the preceding pages - summarised overleaf in an observation checklist) and, at the end of the five minutes, to summarise the arguments that the Speaker has presented.

The task of the Observer is to give feedback to the Listener on how well the rules of good listening have been demonstrated and on how accurate the summary has been. The Observer does not need to give any feedback on the Speaker's performance.

After each of the three rounds, the group can usefully take a couple of minutes to briefly discuss the experience - in particular the way that a viewpoint you do not like may obstruct your ability to listen accurately. This filtering out of unwelcome information is, unfortunately, the reason that so many customer complaints degenerate into horror stories.

## OBSERVER'S CHECKLIST

(S = Speaker; L = Listener)

| BEHAVIOUR TO BE NOTED | DOES IT HAPPEN? | OBSERVER'S COMMENTS |
|---|---|---|
| **1. Listens:** | | |
| ● 80:20 ratio S:L | | |
| ● L does not interrupt | | |
| ● Brings straying S back onto subject | | |
| ● Makes notes | | |
| **2. Checks understanding:** | | |
| ● Asks clarifying questions | | |
| ● Gives reflective summaries | | |
| ● Hears "uncomfortable" things | | |
| **3. Demonstrates listening:** | | |
| ● Eye contact | | |
| ● Body posture | | |
| ● Tone of voice | | |

## OBSERVER'S CHECKLIST

(S = Speaker; L = Listener)

| BEHAVIOUR TO BE NOTED | DOES IT HAPPEN? | OBSERVER'S COMMENTS |
|---|---|---|
| **4. Builds relationship:** | | |
| • Allows S to let off steam | | |
| • Shows can see things from S's point of view | | |
| • Uses S's name | | |
| • Focuses on action for the future | | |
| **5. Diagnostic listening:** | | |
| • Avoids arguing, defending or excusing | | |
| • Admits mistakes and apologises | | |
| • Doesn't jump to conclusions | | |
| • Looks for solutions, not obstacles | | |

56

# ASSERTIVENESS AND GOOD SERVICE

## ASSERTIVENESS AND GOOD SERVICE

# ASSERTIVENESS

Let's start with a note of caution: your personality and all the routine ways in which you respond to the various situations that life throws at you have gradually developed over the years. These patterns of behaviour are well-entrenched by now - they are you. So it would be unrealistic to expect that the next few pages will change you dramatically overnight.  There are three very useful things, though, that you can achieve from this chapter:

- An understanding of a simple framework that describes different kinds of assertive and non-assertive behaviour

- Some ideas for handling the stress caused by other people's behaviour (especially when they are customers)

- Some tips on how you can respond in a constructive way to angry people (especially when they are customers)

# ASSERTIVENESS

Once you understand how you typically react to other people, you are half-way to being able to choose the responses you make.

There are three basic types of behaviour that are of interest here: "passive", "aggressive" and "assertive". What makes each type different from the others lies in your feelings about yourself and your feelings about other people.

It is important that you remember that there are times when either passive or aggressive behaviour may be the best response to a particular situation confronting you. Sometimes, it really is best to bite your tongue and say nothing - and sometimes it is right to fight for your survival.

However, it's also important that you remember that if you are habitually passive you will damage your self-esteem; if you are habitually aggressive you will damage your physical health.

## ASSERTIVENESS
**PASSIVE BEHAVIOUR**

"Passive" behaviour is demonstrated by those people whose view of themselves is that basically they are inferior to others. They think of themselves as less clever, less capable, less attractive to others. Passive people tend towards feelings of fear, nervousness, tension, and sadness. When they find themselves under pressure, their typical response is to give in, to retreat from the perceived threat - "anything for a quiet life". In groups, passive people take a back seat, defer to other people's opinions and decisions, and fail to ask for what they want. Their self-esteem is very dependent upon what other people think of them.

## ASSERTIVENESS
**AGGRESSIVE BEHAVIOUR**

"Aggressive" behaviour is typical of people who feel superior to everyone else. Their self-esteem is derived from putting down other people, either actively by patronising them or using sarcasm, or simply in their mind regarding others as being insignificant. They tend to dominate, demand, and to take what they want. Under pressure, they will attack rather than negotiate. Their most typical feeling is anger or irritation and any conflict is seen as a win/lose equation.

SUPERIOR DOG

(61)

# ASSERTIVENESS
## ASSERTIVE BEHAVIOUR

"Assertive" behaviour is different: learned, not instinctive. It is based upon thinking about yourself and others as being more or less the same in terms of abilities and status: you can do some things that I can't and I can do some things you can't. Assertive people know what they want and can ask for it in a way that does not damage either their own self-esteem or the other person's.

The assertive person does not see the things that he or she is not good at doing as a cause for low self-esteem. Assertive people accept themselves and other people, warts and all.

They are able to feel comfortable and self-confident with others and in control of themselves and the situations they face. Assertive behaviour is thoughtful, not reactive. It is concerned with solving problems rather than scoring points, getting even, or defeating the other person: win/win solutions are sought. It is also assertive behaviour to be able to choose which of the three kinds of behaviour, passive, aggressive, or assertive, is appropriate at any particular moment in time.

## EXERCISE: ANGRY CUSTOMERS

Make a few notes about how you have felt when you have had to deal with an angry and aggressive customer, either on the telephone or face to face. (You may have felt upset, shaken, defensive, a sense of unfairness, anger, you wanted to get your own back, thrown off balance, etc.)

. . . . . . . . . . . . . . . . . . . . . . . . . . . . . . . . . . . . . . . . . . . . . . . . . . . . . . . . . . . . . . . . . . . . . . . . .

. . . . . . . . . . . . . . . . . . . . . . . . . . . . . . . . . . . . . . . . . . . . . . . . . . . . . . . . . . . . . . . . . . . . . . . . .

What do the feelings you have described tell you about your typical mode of responding under pressure?

. . . . . . . . . . . . . . . . . . . . . . . . . . . . . . . . . . . . . . . . . . . . . . . . . . . . . . . . . . . . . . . . . . . . . . . . .

. . . . . . . . . . . . . . . . . . . . . . . . . . . . . . . . . . . . . . . . . . . . . . . . . . . . . . . . . . . . . . . . . . . . . . . . .

Amongst the feelings you have described, are there some which would provide you with a basis for a more assertive response?

. . . . . . . . . . . . . . . . . . . . . . . . . . . . . . . . . . . . . . . . . . . . . . . . . . . . . . . . . . . . . . . . . . . . . . . . .

. . . . . . . . . . . . . . . . . . . . . . . . . . . . . . . . . . . . . . . . . . . . . . . . . . . . . . . . . . . . . . . . . . . . . . . . .

## ASSERTIVENESS AND GOOD SERVICE

# ANGRY CUSTOMERS

Nobody has to listen to abuse. If you can't get the conversation onto a more constructive basis fairly quickly, then you should refer the call to your supervisor. However, there are quite a lot of occasions when tempers get heated and with a bit of thought you can defuse the "aggro" and indeed end up with a contented customer.

The checklist that follows contains some rules for defusing anger.

## ASSERTIVENESS AND GOOD SERVICE

# ANGRY CUSTOMERS
## ACTION CHECKLIST

- Don't take it personally: usually it's the company that they are angry with - and as far as the customer is concerned, you are the company. They don't know you as the nice person your family and friends are familiar with.

- Give the customer space to let off steam before you try to steer them towards a discussion of the facts - they're probably more anxious about the situation than you are. They may have had difficulty getting through to you or may have had previous enquiries mis-handled.

- Take notes and check these back with the customer to demonstrate clearly that you are paying attention and treating the matter seriously.

- Try to keep a calm tone of voice, but if abuse persists pass the call to your supervisor.

- If possible, avoid transferring the call or putting it on hold: get someone to call the customer back promptly. If put on hold, come back on the line at thirty-second intervals to reassure the customer (a minute holding onto an apparently "dead" line can seem like eternity to an already-dissatisfied customer).

## ASSERTIVENESS AND GOOD SERVICE

# ANGRY CUSTOMERS
## STRESS

An uncomfortable side-effect of dealing with angry customers is that their anger often creates stress for the person on the receiving end. Persistent stress can harm your health so it is well worth you learning how to manage any stress you experience. It will help you to stay in assertive mode and to deal more effectively with the situation - and it will leave you feeling better afterwards. To alleviate stress:

- Talk through the problem calls with a supervisor or friend

- After a difficult call, take a moment or two to unwind; don't rush straight into the next difficult call!

- Look after your health, with sensible exercise and eating habits

- Learn breathing exercises that will calm your stress levels

## ASSERTIVENESS
**EXERCISE**

This is an opportunity to apply the ideas of this chapter to your own experience. Start by thinking of a specific situation in which you have found yourself fairly recently - either at work or at home or socially. The key factor when selecting the situation is that you still feel unhappy about the ways in which you responded at the time - you wish you'd "handled it better". Take about ten to fifteen minutes to go through the questions that follow. If possible, find a friend or colleague who is doing the same exercise. Talk through the experiences and how each of you might now respond differently.

## EXERCISE (CONTD): ASSERTIVENESS

1. What triggered the situation you are describing?

. . . . . . . . . . . . . . . . . . . . . . . . . . . . . . . . . . . . . . . . . . . . . . . . . . . . . . . . . . . . . . . . . . . . . . . . . . . . . . . . . .

. . . . . . . . . . . . . . . . . . . . . . . . . . . . . . . . . . . . . . . . . . . . . . . . . . . . . . . . . . . . . . . . . . . . . . . . . . . . . . . . . .

2. What did the other person do and/or say?

. . . . . . . . . . . . . . . . . . . . . . . . . . . . . . . . . . . . . . . . . . . . . . . . . . . . . . . . . . . . . . . . . . . . . . . . . . . . . . . . . .

. . . . . . . . . . . . . . . . . . . . . . . . . . . . . . . . . . . . . . . . . . . . . . . . . . . . . . . . . . . . . . . . . . . . . . . . . . . . . . . . . .

3. How would you characterise the other person's behaviour (passive, aggressive, assertive)? Describe in detail what they did or said that leads you to that characterisation.

. . . . . . . . . . . . . . . . . . . . . . . . . . . . . . . . . . . . . . . . . . . . . . . . . . . . . . . . . . . . . . . . . . . . . . . . . . . . . . . . . .

. . . . . . . . . . . . . . . . . . . . . . . . . . . . . . . . . . . . . . . . . . . . . . . . . . . . . . . . . . . . . . . . . . . . . . . . . . . . . . . . . .

## EXERCISE (CONTD): ASSERTIVENESS

4. At the time, how did you feel about the other person's behaviour?

. . . . . . . . . . . . . . . . . . . . . . . . . . . . . . . . . . . . . . . . . . . . . . . . . . . . . . . . . . . . . . . . . . . . . . . . . . .

. . . . . . . . . . . . . . . . . . . . . . . . . . . . . . . . . . . . . . . . . . . . . . . . . . . . . . . . . . . . . . . . . . . . . . . . . . .

5. How did you respond? (What were your words, actions, body language, etc.?)

. . . . . . . . . . . . . . . . . . . . . . . . . . . . . . . . . . . . . . . . . . . . . . . . . . . . . . . . . . . . . . . . . . . . . . . . . . .

. . . . . . . . . . . . . . . . . . . . . . . . . . . . . . . . . . . . . . . . . . . . . . . . . . . . . . . . . . . . . . . . . . . . . . . . . . .

6. How would you characterise your own behaviour at that time (passive, aggressive, assertive)? Describe in detail what you did or said that leads you to that characterisation.

. . . . . . . . . . . . . . . . . . . . . . . . . . . . . . . . . . . . . . . . . . . . . . . . . . . . . . . . . . . . . . . . . . . . . . . . . . .

. . . . . . . . . . . . . . . . . . . . . . . . . . . . . . . . . . . . . . . . . . . . . . . . . . . . . . . . . . . . . . . . . . . . . . . . . . .

## EXERCISE (CONTD): ASSERTIVENESS

7. What got in the way of you handling the situation more effectively?

. . . . . . . . . . . . . . . . . . . . . . . . . . . . . . . . . . . . . . . . . . . . . . . . . . . . . . . . . . . . . . . . . . . . . . . . . . . . . . . . . . . .

. . . . . . . . . . . . . . . . . . . . . . . . . . . . . . . . . . . . . . . . . . . . . . . . . . . . . . . . . . . . . . . . . . . . . . . . . . . . . . . . . . . .

8. If a similar situation were to occur now, what would you do differently?

. . . . . . . . . . . . . . . . . . . . . . . . . . . . . . . . . . . . . . . . . . . . . . . . . . . . . . . . . . . . . . . . . . . . . . . . . . . . . . . . . . . .

. . . . . . . . . . . . . . . . . . . . . . . . . . . . . . . . . . . . . . . . . . . . . . . . . . . . . . . . . . . . . . . . . . . . . . . . . . . . . . . . . . . .

# EFFECTIVE CUSTOMER COMMUNICATIONS

## EFFECTIVE CUSTOMER COMMUNICATIONS

Communication involves two people - one sending a message and one receiving it. If the message is unclear the wrong actions may follow. At the least, the recipient will be annoyed that the person sending the message cannot manage the courtesy of making their meaning clear.

Always remember that the need for effective communication applies equally to:

● External customers

● Internal customers

## EFFECTIVE CUSTOMER COMMUNICATIONS

## PERFORMANCE STANDARDS

In the section on Performance Standards, you will already have come across two things which contribute to effective communication:

- The "right first time" guideline, which in this context means getting your facts right before putting pen to paper (or finger to keyboard)

- The rule about not passing on errors that you have inherited from someone else

There is another performance guideline to add here:

- Use clear, comprehensible language in all communications, especially written ones

## EXERCISE: YOUR COMMUNICATIONS

List all the various occasions when you need to communicate to internal or external customers in writing (that includes letters, file notes, memos, reports, telephone messages that you pass on, etc.)

1. . . . . . . . . . . . . . . . . . . . . . . . . . . . . . . . . . . . . . . . . . . . . . . . . . . . . . . . . . . . . . . . . . . . . . . . . . . . . . .

2. . . . . . . . . . . . . . . . . . . . . . . . . . . . . . . . . . . . . . . . . . . . . . . . . . . . . . . . . . . . . . . . . . . . . . . . . . . . . . .

3. . . . . . . . . . . . . . . . . . . . . . . . . . . . . . . . . . . . . . . . . . . . . . . . . . . . . . . . . . . . . . . . . . . . . . . . . . . . . . .

4. . . . . . . . . . . . . . . . . . . . . . . . . . . . . . . . . . . . . . . . . . . . . . . . . . . . . . . . . . . . . . . . . . . . . . . . . . . . . . .

5. . . . . . . . . . . . . . . . . . . . . . . . . . . . . . . . . . . . . . . . . . . . . . . . . . . . . . . . . . . . . . . . . . . . . . . . . . . . . . .

6. . . . . . . . . . . . . . . . . . . . . . . . . . . . . . . . . . . . . . . . . . . . . . . . . . . . . . . . . . . . . . . . . . . . . . . . . . . . . . .

7. . . . . . . . . . . . . . . . . . . . . . . . . . . . . . . . . . . . . . . . . . . . . . . . . . . . . . . . . . . . . . . . . . . . . . . . . . . . . . .

8. . . . . . . . . . . . . . . . . . . . . . . . . . . . . . . . . . . . . . . . . . . . . . . . . . . . . . . . . . . . . . . . . . . . . . . . . . . . . . .

9. . . . . . . . . . . . . . . . . . . . . . . . . . . . . . . . . . . . . . . . . . . . . . . . . . . . . . . . . . . . . . . . . . . . . . . . . . . . . . .

10. . . . . . . . . . . . . . . . . . . . . . . . . . . . . . . . . . . . . . . . . . . . . . . . . . . . . . . . . . . . . . . . . . . . . . . . . . . . . .

## EFFECTIVE CUSTOMER COMMUNICATIONS

## WRITTEN COMMUNICATION

There are four main elements to written communication:

- Purpose - what you are aiming to achieve by writing this

- Content - what the substance of your message consists of

- Presentation - the way in which the communication is laid out

- Style - the manner in which you express yourself

## EFFECTIVE CUSTOMER COMMUNICATIONS

# WRITTEN COMMUNICATION
## PURPOSE

We write to other people in order to:

- Give them information they need

- Ask them for information we need

- Make recommendations or suggestions, ie to persuade

- Request action by the other person

Sometimes, only one of these purposes applies; other times a single letter or memo may cover several purposes. When you reflect on your purpose in making the communication you can begin to think about the best way to express what you want (through tone, choice of words, and so on).

## EFFECTIVE CUSTOMER COMMUNICATIONS

## WRITTEN COMMUNICATION
### CONTENT

Before you write something, it's usually helpful to make a quick list of the key points:

- Decide what is essential, what is irrelevant - and leave out the inessentials!

- Decide the order in which the points should be made

- Identify anything which needs particular emphasis or more detailed explanation

## EFFECTIVE CUSTOMER COMMUNICATIONS

# WRITTEN COMMUNICATION
## PRESENTATION

The appearance of written documents can be greatly improved by following a few simple rules:

- Give the document a heading so that the subject is immediately clear - a file reference is not enough

- Space your writing evenly over the available space - don't squash a short text up at the top of the page, leaving lots of blank paper

- Use a new paragraph when you start on a new theme or a new main point of the communication

- If the reader will be asked to comment or act upon various points, it is often helpful to number the paragraphs

- Check any spelling that you are unsure about!

## EFFECTIVE CUSTOMER COMMUNICATIONS

## WRITTEN COMMUNICATION
STYLE

Different people/organisations hold different opinions on what is "good" style. Treat the following guidelines as general principles:

- Plain English is to be preferred to a "flowery" or "literary" style

- Do not use technical jargon and in-house abbreviations that the reader is unlikely to understand; if a technical word has to be used, and you anticipate it may not be understood, give a short clear explanation of the word the first time you use it

- Aim for simple words and short sentences; avoid long, complicated sentences with lots of subsidiary clauses

# WRITTEN COMMUNICATION
## STYLE (contd)

- Get quickly to the point of what you want to say (without being blunt about it, since this may be read as discourtesy)

- Don't be brief at the expense of the reader's understanding; if something needs explaining, do so fully but don't ramble on

- As a rule, avoid ending a sentence with a preposition (from, with, by, to, etc.)

- Try to avoid over-use of words (apart from words like "a" and "the"); a useful rule of thumb is to use a noun or verb not more than once in a sentence and, if possible, not in the next paragraph either; look for alternative words with the same meaning

**EFFECTIVE CUSTOMER COMMUNICATIONS**

# WRITTEN COMMUNICATION
## EXERCISE: THE READABILITY INDEX

The Readability Index enables you to measure your writing style to
see whether you may be making it difficult for your readers
to understand you:

- **First Stage: Length of Sentences**

1. Find something that you have written that contains at least 200
words

2. Excluding commas, count the number of punctuation marks (. : ; ? !)

3. Divide the number of punctuation marks into the number of words
to give an average sentence length. Note that here:

# EFFECTIVE CUSTOMER COMMUNICATIONS

## WRITTEN COMMUNICATION
### EXERCISE: THE READABILITY INDEX (contd)

● **Second Stage: Long Words**

4. Underline all words in your sample that have three or more syllables and add up the total number of these words. Enter it here:

5. Calculate the percentage of long words in your sample. The formula is:

$$\frac{\text{No. of long words}}{\text{No. of words in sample}} \times 100 = \quad \dots\%$$

● **Third Stage: Calculating the Index**

6. Take the average sentence length (para. 3) and the percentage of long words (para. 5) and add them together. This total is your Readability Index. Note it here:

## WRITTEN COMMUNICATION
**EXERCISE: THE READABILITY INDEX (contd)**

An Index of about 30 is typical of everyday conversation and this provides a benchmark that you should aim to improve upon in your writing. (This does not mean you should write just as you speak - conversation is notoriously ungrammatical - but simply that you should aim for a level of written understanding a bit better than that which normal conversation achieves).

If you have arrived at an Index that is under 20, this indicates that you use very short sentences and simple words and it may indicate that your style is a bit too abrupt - rather like a telegram.

## EFFECTIVE CUSTOMER COMMUNICATIONS

## WRITTEN COMMUNICATION
### EXERCISE: THE READABILITY INDEX (contd)

If your Index score totals over 40, then you appear to be padding out your sentences with long words and perhaps with complicated sentence structures. You may be waffling rather than getting to the point. Readers are more likely to have trouble understanding what you are trying to say to them.

Different Index levels are appropriate for different documents. In memos and file notes, a more terse style is acceptable, with the Index down to 15-18. In letters, aim for the range 20-25 and in reports 25-30. Technical and specialised documents are likely to get up into the 35-40 range.

# INTERNAL CUSTOMERS

## INTERNAL CUSTOMERS

# DEFINITION

Everybody (yes, everybody) in an organisation either

- Directly serves customers

OR

- Helps colleagues (your internal customers) who form a chain of customer service within the organisation

At some point that internal chain comes directly into contact with the external customers who buy the goods or services your organisation provides. This means that everybody contributes, directly or indirectly, to the quality of customer care

## INTERNAL CUSTOMERS

# DEFINITION

The idea of an internal customer chain is fine, so long as there are no weak links. Everything works when everyone pulls in the same direction. But it's bad news when "them and us" barriers start to develop, eg:

- Between the sections in a process chain (where different people handle different stages of a document, for instance)

- Between head office and branches

- Between sales and marketing

- Between marketing and manufacturing

This section of the book explores how you can play a positive role in giving your colleagues good internal customer service - and also how you can encourage them to do the same for you.

It offers you the opportunity to be part of the solution, rather than part of the problem...and, anyway, it's much more fun to work in an organisation with a problem-solving culture than one where problems are perpetuated and merely made an excuse for finger-pointing. Soaring like an eagle beats squabbling with the turkeys, any day!

**INTERNAL CUSTOMERS**

# DEALING WITH HISTORY

Even though you may want to change things, you (and your colleagues) do not start off with a clean sheet. There is bound to be an accumulated history of greater or lesser frictions which occurred for reasons that - at the time - seemed valid, but which leave a legacy of touchiness or distrust.

So, first of all, you may want to get off your chest some accumulated irritations about your "internal customers" before you can begin to think more positively about your working relationships. Take ten minutes now for this purpose and complete the "niggles" exercise that follows.

**INTERNAL CUSTOMERS**

# DEALING WITH HISTORY
**EXERCISE**

1. Use the "Niggles Sheet" (see over) to make brief notes about any incidents that you personally have experienced where colleagues have failed to give you the kind of service that you should get as their internal customer - incidents that have made it harder for you to do your job properly:

- It may be things you would prefer them not to do

- It may be things they don't do, but you wish they would

- It may be things that you would like them to do differently

## INTERNAL CUSTOMERS

## DEALING WITH HISTORY
### EXERCISE (contd)

2. If possible, find a partner to discuss your list with - ideally someone who doesn't work in your own section or department, because you want to get a fresh perspective on the problems. Talk through your list and your partner's list:

- Are you suffering from similar problems?

- How much are the problems a matter of where you happen to be standing at the time?

- Is one person's "problem" another person's "correct way to do things"?

- Are the problems being magnified simply because you don't know the individuals you are dealing with (especially over the telephone) so you tend to assume the worst of them?

- Are there misunderstandings because you don't really know what other departments do (or are permitted to do)?

- Which items on your lists ought - at least in principle - to be improvable?

- What could be the benefits to either the organisation or yourselves if these improvements were made?

- What would it take to achieve each of those improvements?

# YOUR PERSONAL NIGGLES SHEET

| Who failed to treat you as their internal customer? | What did they do, do unsatisfactorily or not do at all? | Is it improvable? | What could be the benefits from any improvement? | What would it take to achieve these improvements? |
|---|---|---|---|---|
| | | | | |
| | | | | |
| | | | | |
| | | | | |
| | | | | |
| | | | | |
| | | | | |
| | | | | |

## INTERNAL CUSTOMERS

# INTERNAL NETWORK
## MAPPING

By now you will have some idea of who else is in your internal customer network (at least, you'll have identified the ones who are making things more difficult for you). Now round out the picture by mapping all the people involved. It's helpful to think of your network as consisting of a series of inputs and outputs, with yourself at the centre. Various things get passed to you (information, work tasks, queries, etc.) and you in turn pass various things on to others in the chain, or else directly to external customers.

Use the chart opposite to list who is in your internal customer network - and what it is that gets passed along the service chain. So far as you are able, write in the names of the actual people you deal with. Only use a job title or general description if you don't know their names or if there are a lot of people in the same category (eg "sales assistants"). You may find it helpful to talk to your supervisor about this listing. Note that there is space for up to four inputs and four outputs. You can adjust these numbers to match your own particular situation.

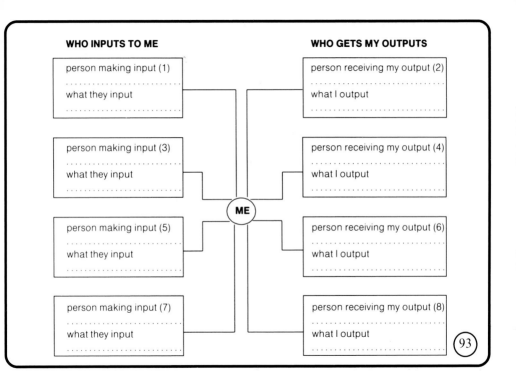

**WHO INPUTS TO ME**

person making input (1)

what they input

person making input (3)

what they input

person making input (5)

what they input

person making input (7)

what they input

**WHO GETS MY OUTPUTS**

person receiving my output (2)

what I output

person receiving my output (4)

what I output

person receiving my output (6)

what I output

person receiving my output (8)

what I output

ME

93

## INTERNAL CUSTOMERS

# INTERNAL NETWORK
## IMPROVEMENTS SHEETS

When you have completed the mapping chart on the previous page, go on to the Improvements Sheets opposite and on the following page. For each of your inputs and outputs, make brief notes on what might improve the way that link in the chain could be handled, by others and by yourself.

Note that most solutions require quite small adjustments in the way people do their jobs - it's not the blockbuster projects, but close attention to small details that adds up to quality of service.

# IMPROVEMENTS SHEET (INPUTS)

| Input number | Changes that would help me to do my job more effectively | What might I be able to do to help make that happen? |
|---|---|---|
| 1. | | |
| 2. | | |
| 3. | | |
| 4. | | |

## IMPROVEMENTS SHEET (OUTPUTS)

| Output number | Changes that would help others to do their jobs more effectively | What might I be able to do to help make that happen? |
|---|---|---|
| 1. | | |
| 2. | | |
| 3. | | |
| 4. | | |

## INTERNAL CUSTOMERS

## INTERNAL NETWORK
### SUPERVISOR'S INPUTS

Arrange a time to discuss your Improvement Sheets with your supervisor or manager. He or she should be able to offer practical comments on how changes might be achieved (and, sometimes, good reasons why they shouldn't be made). Make a note here of the comments and suggestions that you receive:

. . . . . . . . . . . . . . . . . . . . . . . . . . . . . . . . . . . . . . . . . . . . . . . . . . . . . . . . . . . . . . . . . .

. . . . . . . . . . . . . . . . . . . . . . . . . . . . . . . . . . . . . . . . . . . . . . . . . . . . . . . . . . . . . . . . . .

. . . . . . . . . . . . . . . . . . . . . . . . . . . . . . . . . . . . . . . . . . . . . . . . . . . . . . . . . . . . . . . . . .

. . . . . . . . . . . . . . . . . . . . . . . . . . . . . . . . . . . . . . . . . . . . . . . . . . . . . . . . . . . . . . . . . .

. . . . . . . . . . . . . . . . . . . . . . . . . . . . . . . . . . . . . . . . . . . . . . . . . . . . . . . . . . . . . . . . . .

. . . . . . . . . . . . . . . . . . . . . . . . . . . . . . . . . . . . . . . . . . . . . . . . . . . . . . . . . . . . . . . . . .

### INTERNAL CUSTOMERS

## PASSING ON WORK

This has probably already surfaced as an issue somewhere in the work you've done in the last few pages. Even if it hasn't, it is such a central element of the internal customer chain that it is worth listing some guidelines for giving (and receiving) a five-star service when you pass work on to your colleagues.

The kinds of thing that make the difference include:
- Promptness
- Correct information
- Material sent to the correct recipient
- Completeness
- Accuracy
- Clear indication of urgency/importance/other priority
- Realistic promises made by the sender to third parties, so that the work passed on does not dump an unattainable task on the recipient
- Clear, comprehensible, and legible contents

# PERSONAL ACTION PLANNING

## PERSONAL ACTION PLANNING

## PAY-OFF
### USING WHAT YOU HAVE LEARNED

Although it is sometimes interesting to learn new things just for their own sake, the pay-offs from a book like this one only come when you start to use your new knowledge and new skills in your day-to-day work. This is especially true of skills, which need to be practised regularly so that they become second nature, rather than something you have to think about doing deliberately.

So - are you now going out there to transform the way your organisation deals with customers? On your own, the answer is probably "No." But when you and the majority of your colleagues and your supervisors and managers all start to make even small improvements in the quality of internal and external customer service, the cumulative impact soon becomes apparent.

# PERSONAL ACTION PLANNING

## REVIEW
## USING WHAT YOU HAVE LEARNED

This section is where you can look back over the main themes of this book to review what you have learned - and plan what you are going to do with it all. There have been eight main topics:

- Why customer service matters
- What's different about good service?
- Performance standards
- Turn complaints into opportunities
- Listening to customers
- Assertiveness and good service
- Effective customer communications
- Internal customers

Allow about five minutes or so to quickly skim through each of these sections, to remind yourself of the key points. Remember that quality comes from looking after the small details. Pinpoint anything which you feel you could use in your job, either straightaway, or if other things changed to make it possible. Try to link these action points to your Internal Network Map, by asking yourself: "What can I do to improve the quality of my customer service outputs to the people in my network?". Be optimistic - go for it! Use the next page to list as many possible action points as you can.

## ACTION POINTS LIST

(A) Things I could do straightaway:

1. . . . . . . . . . . . . . . . . . . . . . . . . . . . . . . . . . . . . . . . . . . . . . . . . . . . . . . . . . . . . . . . . . . . . .

2. . . . . . . . . . . . . . . . . . . . . . . . . . . . . . . . . . . . . . . . . . . . . . . . . . . . . . . . . . . . . . . . . . . . . .

3. . . . . . . . . . . . . . . . . . . . . . . . . . . . . . . . . . . . . . . . . . . . . . . . . . . . . . . . . . . . . . . . . . . . . .

4. . . . . . . . . . . . . . . . . . . . . . . . . . . . . . . . . . . . . . . . . . . . . . . . . . . . . . . . . . . . . . . . . . . . . .

5. . . . . . . . . . . . . . . . . . . . . . . . . . . . . . . . . . . . . . . . . . . . . . . . . . . . . . . . . . . . . . . . . . . . . .

6. . . . . . . . . . . . . . . . . . . . . . . . . . . . . . . . . . . . . . . . . . . . . . . . . . . . . . . . . . . . . . . . . . . . . .

7. . . . . . . . . . . . . . . . . . . . . . . . . . . . . . . . . . . . . . . . . . . . . . . . . . . . . . . . . . . . . . . . . . . . . .

8. . . . . . . . . . . . . . . . . . . . . . . . . . . . . . . . . . . . . . . . . . . . . . . . . . . . . . . . . . . . . . . . . . . . . .

9. . . . . . . . . . . . . . . . . . . . . . . . . . . . . . . . . . . . . . . . . . . . . . . . . . . . . . . . . . . . . . . . . . . . . .

10. . . . . . . . . . . . . . . . . . . . . . . . . . . . . . . . . . . . . . . . . . . . . . . . . . . . . . . . . . . . . . . . . . . . . .

## ACTION POINTS LIST

(B) Things I could do if other things changed:

1. . . . . . . . . . . . . . . . . . . . . . . . . . . . . . . . . . . . . . . . . . . . . . . . . . . . . . . . . . . . . . . . . . . . . . . . .
What needs to change:

. . . . . . . . . . . . . . . . . . . . . . . . . . . . . . . . . . . . . . . . . . . . . . . . . . . . . . . . . . . . . . . . . . . . . . . . . .

2. . . . . . . . . . . . . . . . . . . . . . . . . . . . . . . . . . . . . . . . . . . . . . . . . . . . . . . . . . . . . . . . . . . . . . . . .
What needs to change:

. . . . . . . . . . . . . . . . . . . . . . . . . . . . . . . . . . . . . . . . . . . . . . . . . . . . . . . . . . . . . . . . . . . . . . . . . .

3. . . . . . . . . . . . . . . . . . . . . . . . . . . . . . . . . . . . . . . . . . . . . . . . . . . . . . . . . . . . . . . . . . . . . . . . .
What needs to change:

. . . . . . . . . . . . . . . . . . . . . . . . . . . . . . . . . . . . . . . . . . . . . . . . . . . . . . . . . . . . . . . . . . . . . . . . . .

4. . . . . . . . . . . . . . . . . . . . . . . . . . . . . . . . . . . . . . . . . . . . . . . . . . . . . . . . . . . . . . . . . . . . . . . . .
What needs to change:

. . . . . . . . . . . . . . . . . . . . . . . . . . . . . . . . . . . . . . . . . . . . . . . . . . . . . . . . . . . . . . . . . . . . . . . . . .

5. . . . . . . . . . . . . . . . . . . . . . . . . . . . . . . . . . . . . . . . . . . . . . . . . . . . . . . . . . . . . . . . . . . . . . . . .
What needs to change:

. . . . . . . . . . . . . . . . . . . . . . . . . . . . . . . . . . . . . . . . . . . . . . . . . . . . . . . . . . . . . . . . . . . . . . . . . .

## OVERCOMING OBSTACLES

Select what you feel are the top two priorities from List (A) and the top three from List (B). (That doesn't mean that the other action points do not matter - simply that you can only tackle so much at once. The other things will still be waiting when you've dealt with the high priorities.) Then use the Force Field Sheet on the following page, to analyse each of these priorities. (You can photocopy the Force Field Sheet, so that you can re-use it for each of your priority tasks.) At some stage, you will probably find it helpful to discuss your analysis with your supervisor.

List (A) First Priority: . . . . . . . . . . . . . . . . . . . . . . . . . . . . . . . . . . . . . . . . . . . . . . . . . .

List (A) Second Priority: . . . . . . . . . . . . . . . . . . . . . . . . . . . . . . . . . . . . . . . . . . . . . . . . . .

List (B) First Priority: . . . . . . . . . . . . . . . . . . . . . . . . . . . . . . . . . . . . . . . . . . . . . . . . . . . .

List (B) Second Priority: . . . . . . . . . . . . . . . . . . . . . . . . . . . . . . . . . . . . . . . . . . . . . . . . . .

List (B) Third Priority: . . . . . . . . . . . . . . . . . . . . . . . . . . . . . . . . . . . . . . . . . . . . . . . . . . .

# FORCE FIELD ANALYSIS SHEET

Priority issue to be analysed: . . . . . . . . . . . . . . . . . . . . . . . . . . . . . . . . . . . . . . . .

Anything that will get in the way of achieving this improvement:

. . . . . . . . . . . . . . . . . . . . . . . . . . . . . . . . . . . . . . . . . . . . . . . . . . . . . . . . . . . . . .

. . . . . . . . . . . . . . . . . . . . . . . . . . . . . . . . . . . . . . . . . . . . . . . . . . . . . . . . . . . . . .
Anything that I can do to weaken the effect of these obstacles (or to by-pass them):

. . . . . . . . . . . . . . . . . . . . . . . . . . . . . . . . . . . . . . . . . . . . . . . . . . . . . . . . . . . . . .

. . . . . . . . . . . . . . . . . . . . . . . . . . . . . . . . . . . . . . . . . . . . . . . . . . . . . . . . . . . . . .
Anything that will help me to achieve this improvement:

. . . . . . . . . . . . . . . . . . . . . . . . . . . . . . . . . . . . . . . . . . . . . . . . . . . . . . . . . . . . . .

. . . . . . . . . . . . . . . . . . . . . . . . . . . . . . . . . . . . . . . . . . . . . . . . . . . . . . . . . . . . . .
Anything that I can do to strengthen these positive factors:

. . . . . . . . . . . . . . . . . . . . . . . . . . . . . . . . . . . . . . . . . . . . . . . . . . . . . . . . . . . . . .

. . . . . . . . . . . . . . . . . . . . . . . . . . . . . . . . . . . . . . . . . . . . . . . . . . . . . . . . . . . . . .
When you have completed your Force Field Analysis, you will probably find it helpful to
discuss your analysis with your supervisor.

## PERSONAL ACTION PLANNING

## SUMMARY

The end of the book...

The beginning of a better way of working...

And a slogan to sum it all up:

- EXCEED customers' expectations

- ENHANCE the reputation of your organisation

- EXCEL in everything you do

# APPENDIX A: SELF ASSESSMENT MATERIALS

## TEST

Here are sixteen questions that you can use to test yourself on how much you have absorbed. The questions offer you a sample of the whole book - they don't cover everything there is to learn. The answers appear on page 112.

1. Why does it matter if the organisation loses even one dissatisfied customer?

. . . . . . . . . . . . . . . . . . . . . . . . . . . . . . . . . . . . . . . . . . . . . . . . . . . . . . . . . . . . . . . . . . .

. . . . . . . . . . . . . . . . . . . . . . . . . . . . . . . . . . . . . . . . . . . . . . . . . . . . . . . . . . . . . . . . . . .

2. Name any Departments or Sections in the organisation which lie outside the Internal Customer Chain.

. . . . . . . . . . . . . . . . . . . . . . . . . . . . . . . . . . . . . . . . . . . . . . . . . . . . . . . . . . . . . . . . . . .

. . . . . . . . . . . . . . . . . . . . . . . . . . . . . . . . . . . . . . . . . . . . . . . . . . . . . . . . . . . . . . . . . . .

3. Briefly describe three performance standards for providing good customer service.

A . . . . . . . . . . . . . . . . . . . . . . . . . . . . . . . . . . . . . . . . . . . . . . . . . . . . . . . . . . . . . . . . .

B . . . . . . . . . . . . . . . . . . . . . . . . . . . . . . . . . . . . . . . . . . . . . . . . . . . . . . . . . . . . . . . . .

C . . . . . . . . . . . . . . . . . . . . . . . . . . . . . . . . . . . . . . . . . . . . . . . . . . . . . . . . . . . . . . . . .

4. State two positive benefits that can be obtained from customers' complaints.

A . . . . . . . . . . . . . . . . . . . . . . . . . . . . . . . . . . . . . . . . . . . . . . . . . . . . . . . . . . . . . . . . .

B . . . . . . . . . . . . . . . . . . . . . . . . . . . . . . . . . . . . . . . . . . . . . . . . . . . . . . . . . . . . . . . . .

## TEST (contd)

5. When you are responding to a complaint, what are four positive things that should underlie the tone of your response to the customer?

A.....................................................................................

B.....................................................................................

C.....................................................................................

D.....................................................................................

6. In handling a complaint, list four kinds of verbal behaviour that you should avoid.

A.....................................................................................

B.....................................................................................

C.....................................................................................

D.....................................................................................

7. What actions should you follow if you find errors in work that has been passed on to you from somebody else?

.......................................................................................

.......................................................................................

8. If you are unable to meet a promised deadline, what should you do?

.......................................................................................

.......................................................................................

## TEST (contd)

9. What two ways can you show a customer (face-to-face) that you really are listening.

A. . . . . . . . . . . . . . . . . . . . . . . . . . . . . . . . . . . . . . . . . . . . . . . . . . . . . . . . . . . . . . . . .

B. . . . . . . . . . . . . . . . . . . . . . . . . . . . . . . . . . . . . . . . . . . . . . . . . . . . . . . . . . . . . . . . .

10. Describe two actions you can take to build up the relationship between yourself and a customer.

A. . . . . . . . . . . . . . . . . . . . . . . . . . . . . . . . . . . . . . . . . . . . . . . . . . . . . . . . . . . . . . . . .

B. . . . . . . . . . . . . . . . . . . . . . . . . . . . . . . . . . . . . . . . . . . . . . . . . . . . . . . . . . . . . . . . .

11. List two important things you can do which help to keep a customer contented, when you are transferring telephone calls.

A. . . . . . . . . . . . . . . . . . . . . . . . . . . . . . . . . . . . . . . . . . . . . . . . . . . . . . . . . . . . . . . . .

B. . . . . . . . . . . . . . . . . . . . . . . . . . . . . . . . . . . . . . . . . . . . . . . . . . . . . . . . . . . . . . . . .

12. What distinguishes assertive behaviour from aggressive or passive styles? Describe in a few words:

A. How assertive people feel about themselves

. . . . . . . . . . . . . . . . . . . . . . . . . . . . . . . . . . . . . . . . . . . . . . . . . . . . . . . . . . . . . . . . . .

B. How assertive people feel about other people

. . . . . . . . . . . . . . . . . . . . . . . . . . . . . . . . . . . . . . . . . . . . . . . . . . . . . . . . . . . . . . . . . .

C. The characteristic behaviour pattern of assertive people

. . . . . . . . . . . . . . . . . . . . . . . . . . . . . . . . . . . . . . . . . . . . . . . . . . . . . . . . . . . . . . . . . .

## TEST (contd)

13.Angry customers tend to cause us stress.  List two actions you can take to manage such stress:

A. . . . . . . . . . . . . . . . . . . . . . . . . . . . . . . . . . . . . . . . . . . . . . . . . . . . . . . . . . . . . . . . . . . . . . . .

B. . . . . . . . . . . . . . . . . . . . . . . . . . . . . . . . . . . . . . . . . . . . . . . . . . . . . . . . . . . . . . . . . . . . . . . .

14.What can you do to defuse the situation with an angry customer?

. . . . . . . . . . . . . . . . . . . . . . . . . . . . . . . . . . . . . . . . . . . . . . . . . . . . . . . . . . . . . . . . . . . . . . . . . .

. . . . . . . . . . . . . . . . . . . . . . . . . . . . . . . . . . . . . . . . . . . . . . . . . . . . . . . . . . . . . . . . . . . . . . . . . .

15.List the four purposes for written communications.

A. . . . . . . . . . . . . . . . . . . . . . . . . . . . . . . . . . . . . . . . . . . . . . . . . . . . . . . . . . . . . . . . . . . . . . . .

B. . . . . . . . . . . . . . . . . . . . . . . . . . . . . . . . . . . . . . . . . . . . . . . . . . . . . . . . . . . . . . . . . . . . . . . .

C. . . . . . . . . . . . . . . . . . . . . . . . . . . . . . . . . . . . . . . . . . . . . . . . . . . . . . . . . . . . . . . . . . . . . . . .

D. . . . . . . . . . . . . . . . . . . . . . . . . . . . . . . . . . . . . . . . . . . . . . . . . . . . . . . . . . . . . . . . . . . . . . . .

16.List four things that you can do in your written documents to improve their presentation.

A. . . . . . . . . . . . . . . . . . . . . . . . . . . . . . . . . . . . . . . . . . . . . . . . . . . . . . . . . . . . . . . . . . . . . . . .

B. . . . . . . . . . . . . . . . . . . . . . . . . . . . . . . . . . . . . . . . . . . . . . . . . . . . . . . . . . . . . . . . . . . . . . . .

C. . . . . . . . . . . . . . . . . . . . . . . . . . . . . . . . . . . . . . . . . . . . . . . . . . . . . . . . . . . . . . . . . . . . . . . .

D. . . . . . . . . . . . . . . . . . . . . . . . . . . . . . . . . . . . . . . . . . . . . . . . . . . . . . . . . . . . . . . . . . . . . . . .

(111)

## TEST MARKING

Award 1 point for each correct answer from the following lists. Your words do not have to be exactly the same:

Q1.
- One dissatisfied customer may spread bad feelings to scores of others
- These people all represent a potential loss of business
- The company depends upon repeat business
- The life-time value of a customer adds up to thousands of pounds

Q2. There are none. Deduct 1 point for each department or section listed

Q3.
- Right first time
- Clear, comprehensible written work
- Previous errors are not passed on
- Promises must be kept
- Provide information other people need at the right time

Q4.
- Opportunity to improve the organisation's work practices
- Opportunity to create a customer who is more satisfied than one who has not needed to complain
- Opportunity to work in a more professional manner

Q5.
- Keep a calm tone of voice
- Always offer to help - never use "it's not my job."
- Emphasise what you can do for them, not negatives
- Focus on corrective action, not history
- Put yourself on their side

Q6.
- Retaliation
- Argument
- Becoming defensive
- Jumping to conclusions
- Blaming other departments or the computer
- Hiding in jargon, or "company policy"

Q7.
- Refer the errors to your immediate supervisor

## TEST MARKING (contd)

**Q8.**
- Notify the person concerned immediately delays become known

**Q9.**
- Maintain eye contact
- Open body posture
- Interested tone of voice

**Q10.**
- Use customer's name
- Give the customer your name
- Sound interested in what they are saying
- Use eye contact
- Use reflective summary to check understanding
- Admit mistakes and apologise

**Q11.**
- Give reason for putting on hold and say for how long
- Transfer calls with summary of details
- Give the customer progress reports on your information-searching

**Q12.**

a.
- My self-esteem is defined by me
- I accept myself and others, flaws and all
- The things that I can't do or don't know about don't harm my self-esteem

b.
- They are more or less the same as me; overall, we come out about equal
- I can do some things they can't, and vice versa
- Their self-esteem is theirs and defined by them

c.
- Comfortable and self-confident
- Competent to deal with situations; in control
- Thinking behaviour
- Effective problem-solving
- Asking for what you want in a way that does not damage your own self-esteem or that of the other person
- Able to decide which of the three behavioural styles is appropriate at any particular moment

# TEST MARKING (contd)

Q13.
- Talk with a friend or supervisor
- Unwind after a difficult call
- Keep healthy through exercise and diet
- Use breathing exercises

Q14.
- Try to avoid transfers or putting on hold
- Get someone to call them back promptly
- Let them blow off steam
- Take notes and check these with the customer to show you're listening
- Politely steer customer to relevant matters
- Keep a calm tone of voice

Q15.
- Give information
- Ask for information
- Make recommendations
- Request action

Q16.
- Give a heading so the subject is clear
- Space your writing evenly on the page
- Use a new paragraph for each major point
- Number the paragraphs
- Check spellings

# APPENDIX B: NOTES FOR MANAGERS & SUPERVISORS

## APPENDIX B:
## NOTES FOR MANAGERS & SUPERVISORS

How Managers Can Make the Difference

- The philosophy of training that underpins this book is that people learn by absorbing new ideas and then trying them out. Managers must therefore be prepared to give their employees the opportunity to test new ways of doing things - and must be tolerant of occasional mistakes during the learning stages.

- To help your employees to learn from this book and to use the skills it describes, managers must actively encourage and reinforce good performance as well as giving constructive feedback when skills fall short of the desired level. Reinforcement covers the range from an encouraging word through to financial rewards linked to annual appraisal.

- Change comes about as a cumulative result of scores or even hundreds of small improvements - all within the capabilities of every person you employ.

- Any individual employee alone is very unlikely to achieve major changes in the quality of customer service in your organisation - management needs to build up a critical mass of people who are pulling in the same direction.

## APPENDIX B:
## NOTES FOR MANAGERS & SUPERVISORS

How Managers Can Make the Difference

- To get the quality of customer service your organisation needs, managers must lead by example - "Do as I do" and not the cynical "Do as I say, not as I do".

- Important initiatives that managers can undertake include:

  Setting up a Quality of Service Council, with members from all levels in the organisation

  Creating small Quality Action teams, mainly drawn from lower level employees, to analyse work problems and recommend improvements

  Identifying performance standards both for the organisation as a whole and for individual departments or sections

  Presenting a clear message about the organisation's strategy and priorities

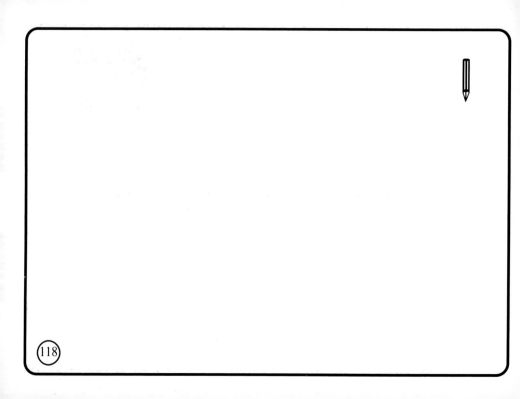

# APPENDIX C: NOTES FOR TRAINERS

# APPENDIX C: NOTES FOR TRAINERS

## WORKSHOPS

The contents of this book can be readily adapted to provide a one-day trainer-led workshop. The individual exercises and tasks in the book can be easily employed by the trainer in small groups and a timetable plan for a one day workshop follows:

| Session No. & Duration | Cumulative elapsed time | Session Content |
|---|---|---|
| 1. 10 | 10 | Presenter: Introduction to the day |
| 2. 05 | 15 | Quiz: "How Customer-Friendly Are You?" |
| 3. 30 | 45 | Exercise "When You Were the Customer...," and group discussion "What is Customer Service about?" |
| 4. 25 | 1-10 | Group discussion: "How Can We Turn Complaints Into Opportunities For Good Customer Service?" |
| | 1-30 | Tea/coffee break |
| 5. 20 | 1-40 | Presentation: "Performance Standards & Customer Service" |
| | | |
| | | |
| 5. 10 | | |
| 6. 40 | 2-20 | Exercise on Listening Skills |
| 7. 60 | 3-20 | Group discussion, and exercise on "Assertiveness" |
| | 4-15 | Lunch (12.50-13.45) |
| 8. 55 | 4-55 | Discussion, and exercise on use of "Clear English" |
| 8. 40 | | |
| 9. 30 | 5-25 | Group discussion, and Brainstorming Exercise: "Passing on work to colleagues" |
| | 5-40 | Tea/coffee break (14.55-15.10) |
| 10. 15 | 6-10 | Personal action planning + group feedback (with particular emphasis on personal action planning to help your internal customers) |
| 10. 30 | | |
| 11. 15 | 6-25 | Customer Service Skills: a summary; plus questions |
| 12. 20 | 6-45 | Assessment Session |
| 13. 05 | 6-50 | Close of workshop |

**APPENDIX C: NOTES FOR TRAINERS**

# WORKSHOPS

**Objectives of a Customer Service Skills Workshop:**

1. To ensure a common base level of competence in customer service skills by all employees. These skills include:

   - listening
   - assertiveness
   - communications, especially the use of clear English
   - effective passing on of work to colleagues
   - handling complaints constructively

2. To reinforce understanding of who each employee's internal and/or external customers are

3. To reinforce any other quality improvements taking place concurrently within the organisation

4. To encourage constructive problem-solving through prompt personal action by every employee

# WORKSHOPS

**Some notes on running the workshop:**

You will need one copy of this book for each participant to use as a workbook during the course. Your presentation will benefit if you prepare a number of overhead projector slides beforehand, to cover the key points you will be discussing. You will probably also wish to customise the discussions and activities so draw upon examples that are specific to your own organisation.

Prepare and rehearse ahead of time. Your credibility is greatly enhanced when you can run the workshop without constant reference to notes or prompt cards - though do keep these for emergencies (even the most experienced can dry up sometimes!).

The steps you should follow when running each stage of the workshop are:
- Explain why they're doing the exercise/having the discussion
- Direct them to the relevant part of the book
- Explain the steps the participants should follow
- Debrief each session, especially drawing out points that help them to transfer ideas back into their work
- Bridge to the next stage

## APPENDIX C: NOTES FOR TRAINERS

# WORKSHOPS

**More notes on running the workshop:**

It is very important that the trainer's choice of language, tone of voice, body language, etc. all convey a clear commitment to the purposes of the workshop. If you've reservations about anything, sort it out before you get in front of a workshop group!

Be prepared to adjust to differences of experience in your audience. Be sensitive to indications of different learning styles and varying depths of work experience amongst your audience. The trainer's task lies in creating opportunities for people to learn (for themselves) and to internalise new ways of doing things, rather than simply teaching "right answers".

When you are conducting group sessions it is always preferable to go round the group randomly (not "creeping death"!) asking for comments or answers to questions. Encourage other participants to correct or expand on answers. Use comments and answers to questions as a trigger to discussion of the implications for customer service. Encourage people to think for themselves about the application of the general point to their specific jobs.

## APPENDIX C: NOTES FOR TRAINERS

# WORKSHOPS

**More notes on running the workshop:**

Remember that the average span of attention, without a change of activity (eg a change from listening to doing), is about 20 minutes! Also remember that 80% of a lecture is forgotten within 24 hours, unless it is reinforced by other training activities.

Lastly, don't forget to emphasise the very important message that quality improvements come, not from a few great leaps forward, but from hundreds or thousands of small improvements of the kind that your audience can themselves make.

## About the Author

**Tony Newby** BA, MA has undertaken consultancy and training assignments both with multi-nationals and with growing companies, as well as with local and central government. He has experience in: design and delivery of client-specified training; culture change and management development; assertiveness; creativity; effective listening; evaluation of training effectiveness; computer skills for the computer-shy; and, of course, customer service quality.

His books on management training topics have been published in the UK and USA.

© Tony Newby 1991

This edition published in 1991 by Management Pocketbooks Ltd
14 East Street, Alresford, Hants. SO24 9EE
Reprinted 1995, 1997, 1998
Printed in England by Alresford Press Ltd., Alresford, Hants. SO24 9QF

# ORDER FORM

## Your details

Name _____

Position _____

Company _____

Address _____

_____

_____

_____

Telephone _____

Facsimile _____

VAT No. (EC companies) _____

Your Order Ref _____

## Please send me:

| | | No. copies |
|---|---|---|
| The Customer Service | Pocketbook | |
| The _____ | Pocketbook | |
| The _____ | Pocketbook | |
| The _____ | Pocketbook | |
| The _____ | Pocketbook | |
| The _____ | Pocketbook | |
| The _____ | Pocketbook | |

### Order by Post

**MANAGEMENT POCKETBOOKS LTD**
14 EAST STREET ALRESFORD HAMPSHIRE SO24 9EE UK

### Order by Phone, Fax or Internet

Telephone: +44 (0)1962 735573
Facsimile: +44 (0)1962 733637
E-mail: pocketbks@aol.com
http://members.aol.com/pocketbks

MANAGEMENT
POCKETBOOKS